I0757970

# Idiots From Hell

## How to Stop Them Ruining our Lives

Pierre A. Kandorfer, Ph.D.

Dedicated to all people who cherish and defend the US
Constitution and US Bill of Rights

# Chapters

Political correctness

## The idiots in our culture
Hollywood-style maniacs dominate our culture
The poison of the falsehood
Even smart people make stupid choices
Dangers of a collective thinking
Cultural indicators
No more Ten Commandments
Why is the culture so important?
Idiotic sitcoms and reality TV dumbing us down
Most ridiculous student demands

## The idiots in our media
Media research proves a blatant dishonesty
Mind manipulation and manufactured stories
Idiots, liars, and journalists
The "whores" of our free speech
The propaganda wars
The idiots on the web
Social media: The best and worst at the same time

## How to maintain our sanity despite idiots
Discover who your enemies are
Think outside of the box
Think positively
Find humor in your life
Don't get dragged into other people's fights
Smile and make other people smile
Manage your stress
Be an optimist
Learn patience

# The idiots - and what they can teach us about life
A positive approach to negative people

## References

*"Life is tough, but it's even tougher if you are stupid." (John Wayne)*

## The idiotic utopia

Throughout the history of human civilization, there were always many stupid, unreasonable, mean, violent, annoying, and deeply egotistical people around. They always were a minority and did not bother the rest of humanity much at all.

Nowadays, however, our "modern lifestyle" with "me first" attitude, increased the number of idiots of all sorts to an almost unbearable level.

Not just in the society at large, politics, and all aspects of our culture. Even among our acquaintances, best friends, and also within our own family, we face weird attitudes we can only summarize as "idiotic."

Behavioral research proves that the amount of silly, deceptive, self-centered, and totally unreasonably acting people with a "profound intellectual disability condition" is on the rise.

Their total misjudgment of the world, unreasonable expectations, foul language, and idiotic antics accumulate to an agonizing frustration for all of us. Idiots from hell!

What is the definition of an "idiot"? It is, among other factors, a stupid, unreasonable, deranged person with a major behavioral disorder.

**Mostly it's just stupidity**

Our world is populated with people with radically different levels of intelligence. Even though most humans consider themselves as some kind of "smart" or even intelligent, many of them have actually a very low IQ.

Most idiotically behaving humans are usually somehow dumb, and their low intelligence causes all kinds of problems for them. They can't handle their own problems, and they become a problem for society themselves.

Usually, there are many fundamental differences between smart and dumb people. They always behave very differently.

- Stupid people always blame others for their own mistakes. They are virtually always unprofessional and unreasonable.
- Stupid people practically never take responsibility for their own failures.

- Stupid people's brains act and react differently to mistakes than regular population, Michigan State University neurological research showed.
- Stupid people insist to be always right. They argue endlessly without any logical or reasonable point.


- Stupid people always react to conflicts with anger and aggression. The Michigan State University researchers found a very strong correlation between aggression and low IQ.
- Stupid people mostly ignore the needs and feelings of other people. While intelligent people easily
  empathize with other individuals, stupid ones rarely can.
- Stupid people consider themselves "better than others" under most unrealistic circumstances.
  Intelligent people often motivate and help others, stupid people are always afraid of being overshadowed by others.

**Types of stupidity**

There are many types of utopian fiction we can only call "idiotic."

- Ecological utopia
- Economical utopia
- Political utopia

- Spiritual utopia
- Science and tech utopia
- Ecological dystopia
- Economical dystopia
- Political dystopia

All these utopian ideas might be good entertainment in science fiction movies, but they don't have anything in common with reality.

**The utopian world without borders**

One of the most naïve and unworkable ultra-leftwing political projects is the international advocacy group "Pueblo Sin Fronteras" (People without borders). They are a major force behind out illegal immigration and fundamentally demand to eradicate all borders between countries and let everybody move wherever desired.

While the idea of "people without borders" makes a perfect sense in a romantic ferry-tale for children, in the daily reality it is a nightmare for every civilized country.

No society of any kind has ever survived by letting every potential enemy uncontrolled into the country, taking advantage of a well-organized political and social system.

Any uncontrolled, illegal big-scale immigration automatically leads to political and social chaos, in addition to billions of dollars spent on the overburdened welfare system.

Organizations like Pueblo Sin Fronteras know this very well because political and social chaos is their goal. Like all Marxists, they are aware that they can best control the masses by creating unrests of any kind.

That's why all communists call for a revolution in order to take over the political power. The communist October revolution in the Soviet Union happened exactly the same way.

As naively "idealistic" some of their utopists might be, they pose a grave danger to our democratic system and the Constitution. No one who really loves freedom and liberty can at the same time like such radical utopian beliefs.

This type of people makes our life miserable, and we must find a way how to handle them.

**"Perfect world" turning into a "living hell"**

There are millions of idiots in the world who are still dreaming of "perfect world order." Of course, it is supposed to be a Marxist dream, finally the "perfect form of Marxism."

The experience of the last one hundred years, when communism never worked, doesn't apply. "Marxism has never been done right, next time we'll correct all mistakes," utopists argue.

The idea of a perfect human society has many facets. For countless people, it's their illusion of freedom, peace, and justice.

But is this really freedom? Freedom means accepting things you might dislike. This kind of a world is automatically less perfect. The utopia, however, actually means a loss of freedom "for the better good."

In order to reach the perfect utopia, you must first take people's basic rights away. You must eliminate the free speech, Second Amendment, and religious freedoms.

This makes the world "less controversial," but is this a world we want to live in? No one who loves the freedom and personal liberty wants the utopia. Specifically, any kind of Marxist utopia is not compatible with the democracy, free speech, US Constitution, and Bill of Rights. No exceptions!

## The idiots denying reality

The personality profile of an arrogant, ignorant, mean, stupid, unreasonable person is very telling and easy to distinguish. Idiots don't just have constant problems with most people around them, they have, first of all, dramatic problems with themselves. They are all terribly dysfunctional without even knowing or admitting it. What is typical for them?

- Bully, selfish, arrogant, annoying
- Display a behavioral disorder and bad judgment
- Attracted to glittering, external rewards such as fame, money, praise, and status
- Thrive on gossips and hearsays
- Exaggerate own strengths, underestimate others
- Never apologize for anything and always invent own explanations
- Never admit to being wrong
- Never want to be challenged

- Their attitude always leads to major inaccuracies, misjudgments, and terrible frustrations
- Love to be praised
- Tend to be short-tempered
- Rush to judgment before all facts are known
- Appear to be outspoken, brave, but can also retaliate with a full force of their pit-bull style of vengeance
- In contrast to their behavior, they mostly hide their cowardice
- They pretend to be strong, but actually are mostly very fragile

Why are so many people so mean, unreasonable, aggressive, judgmental, and stupid? Psychologists have an extensive explanation for their behavior. They act unreasonably and therefore stupidly because they are trying to overcome a series of own problems.

A psychological analysis of an idiotic personality uncovers a long row of deficiencies. They are the actual reason for their erratic behavior, which is supposed to deflect from their own inferiority.

Dealing with rude, unfriendly, intimidating, and disrespectful people can be very harmful to our own emotional well-being. If we are not emotionally stable and are at the same time in a hostile intimate relationship, a warning is due.

There are many reasons why people behave erratically.

- They suffer under poor communications skills
- They dislike you or hold a grudge against you
- They feel better when they put other people down
- They anticipate their aggressiveness appears them more powerful
- They were raised in a bad family environment
- They don't respect other people
- They have a poor self-awareness and social awareness
- They disagree with you politically or ideologically
- They are often yuppie-style snobs
- They are just having a bad day

**The reasons for a denial**

Nothing happens without a reason. Often, we are flabbergasted watching people denying the most obvious, logical facts imaginable. We just can't comprehend why some people just don't get it.

The reason is not a rational conclusion based on facts. Just the opposite. Their denial is based on emotions they can't handle.

- Don't argue with them by providing facts, logic or reason
- Figure out what their emotions, goals, and values are leading them to their assumptions
- Try to understand their emotions, as irrational they might be, in order to build trust

- If you reach a point when they start trusting you, try to carefully lead them away from their belief
- Then, try now to present them the logical, fact-based explanation of the problem

## The idiots acting like idiots

We encounter stupid, unreasonable, mean, crazy, and deranged people with all kinds of behavioral disorders and intellectual disabilities everywhere. In short, we call most of them idiots. We can't stand them because they make our lives miserable.

Idiots come in all shapes, types, and forms. They are extremely frustrating to all, and they sometimes even manage to make us doubt our own sanity.

Wow! Who is actually the crazy one? Are they out of their mind – or it's me going nuts?

Never mind how do you answer this question, it never hurts to examine your own sanity. If you consider yourself some kind of "normal," this should not take a lot of time. Usually, this type of "self-examination" produces a quick result.

But, it's them! But how can we handle them without becoming angry, miserable, and depressed?

Our first impulse is to talk to somebody. The second desire is to the gym or straight to the next bar. However, this doesn't solve our problem at all.

First of all, we must maintain our own sanity and get the right mindset whenever we must deal with idiots. There are some general rules on how to adjust your attitude toward their irrationality.

- Expect nothing - and you won't be disappointed
- Don't offer them any information or "help" because they will despise it
- Don't take it personally - because it's not
- Try to protect yourself by visualizing your own body isolated in a "bubble" such as mother's womb where nobody can hurt you

Dealing with unreasonable people is a very complex, frustrating, frightening, and sometimes maddening problem. Psychologists developed an approach to this kind of dilemma, quite not un-similar to approaching a vicious dog.

- Listen first
- Try to stay calm
- Don't instantly judge
- Maintain respect for others
- Look for their maybe hidden needs
- Look for help

- Don't demand compliance
- Ask them to "tell more" in order to understand the point better
- Your smiling might be considered offending.
- Don't respond to anger with anger
- Don't argue to convince them
- Saying "I am sorry" might help to increase tensions
- Set your own limits
- Trust your own instincts
- There is never a "one size fits all" solution
- Debrief with somebody you trust
- Discharge your stress in order to get rid of too much adrenaline
- Believe in yourself and take some credit for solving an uncomfortable dispute

**Why do we differ so dramatically?**

*You cannot trust your eyes if your imagination is out of focus (Mark Twain).*

Whatever we do or not do, whatever we think, value or hate, how we behave and whatever we believe in or not in our life, mainly depends on one thing: our worldview. An oversimplified analogy might be: Whenever we change our eyeglasses, our view of things around us changes because our eyeglasses determine what we are able to see or not to see.

Everybody has a worldview. Rich or poor, smart or stupid, believer or non-believer. All things in our life depend on our worldview. Derived from the German word "Weltanschauung," it refers to a belief system holding all significant concepts of our life such as God, cosmos, knowledge, behavior, values, humanity and history. It is like a kind of a grand perspective of our world and our life.

In more scientific terms, worldview is a mental structure forming our ultimate beliefs. As Reasons.org outlines, it provides a general context for life, including a vision of what we consider "authentic" or "real."

According to philosophers, a worldview should answer the following most important questions of our life:

- Ultimate reality: What kind of God, if any, in fact, exists?
- External reality: Is there anything beyond the cosmos?
- Knowledge: What can be known – and how can anyone know it?
- Origin: Where did I come from?
- Identity: Who am I?
- Morals: How should I live?
- Values: What should I consider of greatest worth?
- Predicament: What is humanity's fundamental problem?
- Resolution: How can humanity's problems be solved?
- Past/Present: What is the meaning and direction of history?

- Destiny: Will I survive the death of my body and if so, in what state?

The answers to such question can provide the focus and purpose of your life as well as logical coherence and reference to reality.

Our worldview is much like an optical perspective. The view changes if we switch our position from left to right, from a low position to a bird's eye view. This analogy applies basically to all views and beliefs in our life.

Therefore, we are confronted with countless "perspectives" to virtually all questions of personal and public life.  If we are lucky, our media outlets offer us "different viewpoints" to many questions we might be interested in.

Some zealots, again and again, want to suggest that these perspectives from their worldview present their "version of the truth."

The truth, however, does not have any "versions." Truth is the truth. Period. Deviation of the truth is just an opinion of a person who wants to bend the actual truth in order to promote their own ideology.

Depending on the history, culture, personal background, ideology, and religious beliefs, there are many worldviews we encounter every day.  There are two basic worldview groups clashing with each other dramatically: religious believers and non-believers.

The historically, politically and socially most significant are the Marxist, Muslim, Atheist and Christian worldview.

## Islamic Worldview

The objective of Islamic worldview is to provide the Muslims with the knowledge and explanation of the world as explained in the Koran, to teach people how to achieve main values of Islam, and to establish the fundamental ethical concepts of human existence.

- Everything in the Islamic worldview is based in Allah (Muslim "God"), Mohammed (their prophet) and Koran ("word of Allah")
- "Islam" means total submission to Allah. No exceptions
- Islam is not just a "religion," it is a comprehensive, totalitarian way of life, dictating all aspects of personal, public, political and social life

From the standpoint of Western civilization, democracy, and human rights, Islam is hardly compatible with any Western values, morals, and principles.

This "clash of civilizations" is grounded in the Sharia, the highly controversial Muslim law that, according to Koran, supersedes all other laws, social customs and government regulations all over the world.

"There is no other law but Sharia," Islamic scholars strictly declare. Muslims are told that they must adhere to only one law: Sharia.

The Sharia-based Islamic worldview contains a long series of "laws" that we might consider cynical, inhuman or even barbaric. All this is "normal" for Muslims. Here is a short list of Sharia strict requirements enforced for every Muslim:

- Criticizing or denying Allah is punishable by death
- Criticizing or denying the Koran or parts of it is punishable by death
- Criticizing or denying Mohammed is punishable by death
- A Muslim leaving Islam is punishable by death
- A Non-Muslim leading a Muslim away from Islam is punishable by death
- A Non-Muslim marrying a Muslim woman is punishable by death
- Muslim men can marry and have sex with an infant girl as young as nine years old
- Female genital mutilation (FGM, cut out of the female clitoris) is a must for Muslim girls
- A Muslim woman can have only one husband, but a man can have up to four wives
- A Muslim man can divorce his wife anytime, but a wife needs a husband's consent to divorce
- A Muslim wife loses her custody for all children over six years of age

- A Muslim man can beat his wife anytime for insubordination
- If a Muslim woman claims to have been raped, she needs four male witnesses to prove it
- A raped woman cannot testify in court against the rapist
- In court proceedings, woman's testimony carries half of the weight of a man
- Muslim females always inherit just half of what males inherit
- A Muslim woman is not allowed to drive a car
- A Muslim woman cannot speak to a man who is not her husband or relative
- A Muslim woman must prepare every meal containing the meat of animals barbarically slaughtered by "Halal"

The Islamic worldview documents perfectly that "normal" is what your worldview considers "normal." Muslims are supposed to use the Koran prescribed technique of Taqiyya towards non-Muslims, which encompasses lying and deception if this helps to advance Islam.

Again, the entire Muslim worldview is based on these Islamic principles. This explains drastically, why there are not many "moderate" Muslims around, and why Muslims are not allowed to assimilate into any other culture.

As leading Islamic scholars boldly demand, the purpose of Muslim refugees in the West is not to "assimilate," but to "breed" as many children as possible in order to advance Islam worldwide.

This is exactly what happens in all countries accepting unlimited Muslim immigration. With virtually no exception, they remain in their own enclaves, maintaining their own culture and practicing Islam as prescribed by Koran.

Even when they live in the US for decades and are naturalized citizens, they practically always identify themselves as "Muslims first." This is the deciding factor for their worldview that our civilization is clashing with.

**Atheistic Worldview**

In short, for atheists and evolutionists, there is no God, no afterlife, nothing supernatural. Everything is "naturally" explainable. By embracing the materialism popularized by the enlightenment period, they shut the door of spiritualism, knowledge, science, and technology.

For atheists, the verdict is final. No more search for truth, no more research, no more possibility that there is more than matter, flesh and accumulation of chemical substances as the building block of our life and the entire universe. No "design work" for the most complex process imaginable is necessary.

Clinging to the "big bang" and evolution theory, claiming basically that "everything came out of nothing," puts atheists in total contradiction to countless scientific findings and natural laws of physics – in addition to the Bible. *(Extensive explanation is available in my book "No more doubt – Science confirms the Bible)*

As atheists' poster child Richard Dawkins expresses, the purpose of atheism is to "free children from indoctrination by the religion of their parents and their community." Dawkins believes that "there is only the nature there is…" Despite countless contradictions, many atheists even claim that their worldview is "scientific". Their basic belief is:

- Everything is material. Just matter. People are their own "Gods." People make their own rules, morals, and values.
- Under this philosophy, only people themselves decide whether acts like murder, lying, stealing or hurting others are "bad" or not. There is no higher authority than us.
- The logical consequence of an atheistic worldview is that there are no Ten Commandments for them. No rules, morals, and values as described in the Bible.

What does this mean? This means that for atheists the main moral principles and guidelines of our Judeo-Christian culture don't apply. For most people believing in the atheistic worldview, there is no "good' and "bad" – just "different." This results in dramatic consequences in their character and social behavior.

Nobody claims that all atheists are necessarily "bad people," but they all struggle to find their own morality and social attitude. They lack any kind of moral roots Christians have in their spirituality, God and Ten Commandments.

**Marxist Worldview**

Lenin himself unmistakably characterizes the Marxist worldview: "Religion is opium for the people. Religion is a sort of spiritual booze…" Communists are atheists, with some exception such as "Liberation theology" in South and Middle America where Christianity is only used as a deceptive tool to reach originally very religious people in this part of the world.

According to Karl Marx, God "does not, cannot and must not exist." In a Marxist worldview, God is considered an "impediment and enemy to a materialistic, socialistic way of life." Following the communist theory, "the humanity is God." "We created God in our own image. We created a religion to worship ourselves," Marx states.

As proclaimed in the Communist Manifesto (1848), Marxism totally reflects atheism. As a Marxist, you must be an atheist, propagator of a "God-free" world. Socialists and communists also claim that their materialistic worldview is "scientific" (refer to the chapter about Evolution).

Generally speaking, the Marxist worldview is virtually identical with the atheist worldview, with the exception of its communist agenda.

An atheist does not have to be a Marxist, but a communist must be an atheist.

On the basis of this worldview, everything looks different than through the glasses of a Christian society. The Marxist's worldview is based on an unquestionably dominating big government in all parts of life. The state knows better what is good or bad for you. The state makes all-important decisions in your life. The people are "not smart enough" to decide what to learn, what to buy, what to eat, how to behave and what and how to think.

- Your personal freedoms are meaningless. You must sacrifice them for "the better good" of society. The "collective" is important, and the collective must adhere to all principles of socialism.

- No free speech, no free thinking, no free press, no free opinion. These are Marxist's ideals, and there is no way around it. In short: Marxist dictatorship is maintained only by brutal force, deception, and corruption of human minds.

This worldview, of course, constitutes a major conflict with a free society as declared in our Constitution and our Bill of Rights.

## Christian Worldview

The biblical worldview is rooted in the infallible word of God. If you believe in the word of the Bible, this is the foundation of everything you believe, think, say and do.

Just from the biblical perspective, it is hard not to believe what the Bible says. Here are just a few proven historical facts:

- The Bible has been written by about forty authors during more than a thousand-year period and is by far still the most consistent and structured piece of literature ever printed. The most advanced computer systems can't emulate this.

- The Bible contains about eight hundred predictions. Many of them have been proven and happened exactly as predicted. Among hundreds of other things, Jesus' birth, life, and death was predicted in detail hundreds of years before his birth.

- Over 25,000 archeological discoveries confirm the accuracy of the Bible.

- Many highly important aspects of the Jewish Exodus events in Egypt have been confirmed by Egyptian hieroglyphs – hardly a pro-Christian information source.

George Barna conducted a survey about the Christian worldview with the following questions:

- Do absolute moral truths exist?
- Does the Bible define absolute truth?
- Did Jesus live a sinless life?
- Is God the all-powerful and all-knowing creator of the universe, and does he still rule it today?
- Is salvation a gift from God and cannot be earned?
- Is Satan real?
- Does a Christian have a responsibility to share his or her faith with other people?
- Is the Bible accurate in all of its teachings?

Try to answer these questions as honestly and truthfully you can. This will surely help you to find out where you stand with your worldview.

The Christian worldview is much more than a simple belief system. It is a complete and integrated framework, giving you the ability to see the world from your standpoint. It consists of the following elements:

- Theologically, Christian worldview is the affirmation of the existence of a highly intelligent, powerful, just, loving and awesome God. It is rooted in Genesis verse 1:1 stating, "In the beginning, God created the heaven and the earth." This is the foundation of everything Christians believe.

- 

- Philosophically, the Christian worldview is based on the belief that Jesus Christ is the word and mind of God. This doctrine claims that it is without exception consistent with findings in science, history and personal experience, which the dialectical materialism never can achieve.

- Ethically, the Christian worldview is exceptionally important because it confirms that God's moral nature is absolute and unchanging. Like the Ten Commandments, the Bible tells us the clear difference between good and evil.

- Scientifically, the Christian worldview proves that the Bible and the creationism are historically and scientifically correct. Contrary to the atheistic, naturalistic worldview of the evolution theory, hundreds of Bible statements have been proven through the laws of nature scientifically.

- Psychologically, the Christian worldview helps to understand the mind-body dualism and its true spiritual understanding. Only this perspective addresses the innermost concerns of an individual. Only through Christian psychology can people recognize their inner selves as well as their mistakes and sinfulness.

- Sociologically, the Christian worldview offers the proposition that the individual and the social order of our society are important to God, mankind, and humanity. Importantly, God ordained the social institutions of family and church in order to teach love, respect, discipline, work, and community.

- Legally, the Christian worldview states that our laws consist of both natural law and divine law as an expression of a righteous and loving God. The Christian concept of human rights is derived from the biblical doctrine of man's creation in the image of God.

- Politically, the Christian worldview is extremely important because it demands moral responsibility in all political actions. It recognizes the state as a God-ordained institution, but the Bible calls for a limited government. Therefore, the government has limited obligations – never totalitarian powers.

- Economically, the Christian worldview says that the "free enterprise" system is the most compatible with Christianity. This is because the Bible establishes a concept of justice, protecting the rights of individuals from infringement of others and containing important basic checks and balances in order to guarantee human rights.

What is your worldview? The answer will ultimately decide what you consider "normal" or "idiotic," whether you are happy or unhappy with our political system and our society.

This will decide what or who you like and what or who you don't.

## The annoying idiots - and how to stop them

You can fight many things in life, but you can't fight stupidity. It is extremely frustrating to deal with people who "just don't get it" because they might not be bright enough.

Such people might not be what we call straight forward "stupid". Plainly described, their intellectual capacity is limited. There are millions of them all over in the world.

Some of them are just not as intelligent as you are. Others might have the necessary brain potential but never had the opportunity to be properly educated.

Looking at them with condescension from your standpoint of elitist superiority is surely not the appropriate thing to do.

Many of "less bright" people can't help themselves because they are either intellectually or mentally limited, and there is nothing they can do about, or maybe never had the chance of getting the appropriate education.

Unfortunately, there is nothing we can initiate to change their knowledge and intelligence. On the other side, there is a lot we can do how we interact with them and how to perceive them.

Some small changes in our communications style and our attitude might make our interaction with "less intelligent people" much less frustrating for us - and much less humiliating for them.

## Be courteous

Don't call the intellectually impaired people out. The worst thing you can do is to let them feel you consider them dumb. This will only make them angry, which might end the entire conversation.

If you are really frustrated, don't let them feel that. If you need some kind of result, try to offer them help in understanding the problem you must discuss with them.

## Look for their talents or strengths

The person might appear to you as totally "dumb," and you don't know what to do. Everybody has some talents or strengths. Try to find them and tell them you value their skills.

Compliment such people and encourage them to use their talents and strengths in life. This is not only helping you - but also them.

**Be respectful and empathetic**

Always try to treat people the way you want to be treated by others yourself. Being respectful to less fortunate or less intelligent people will surely go a long way to ensure the necessary positive energy you both need.

Never start arguing, even though you might be absolutely sure that you are right and the person opposite of you is wrong. Try to be empathetic, try to see the world from the perspective of their eyes.

Find a polite way to convince them that your version of the matter is right – without letting them feel that they are wrong.

**Think cautiously**

Try to be very careful before initiating any negative consequences for the "less smart" people you have to deal with. Don't express much of anything about their limited intellectual capability to people who might use this information against them.

Stick to the facts if you decide that you must report them. Always consider if this would really benefit you and whether this is the right thing to do if you take advantage of the situation.

## Don't instantly judge people

People may speak, act and react differently than you, but this might not automatically be a result of low intelligence. Try to avoid judgments right away just because somebody speaks slowly and act strangely. Some people with disabilities are highly intelligent, they just can't perform the way we do.

**Don't overstate your own intelligence**

As much as your intellectual ability is a very positive factor, it might also be sometimes counter-productive if you overstate it or become arrogant.

Never forget that some people need a lot more time to learn or comprehend a complicated matter than you. They just have to spend more time to get it, but this does not automatically make them dumb.

**Never forget your own weaknesses**

We all encounter people from various social and educational levels all the time. It is very advisable not to jump to any conclusion about the smartness of other individuals before you thoroughly examine the facts and self-reflect.

Another important factor is the style of communication with other persons. Most of the "people persons" are good communicators, as Ronald Reagan used to be, but the incapability of some people not being able to compete with your perfect communications style does not mean that they are stupid.

**Never display your cerebral predominance**

You might be extremely intelligent and prime authority in a specific subject, but it does not do you any good if you purposely display your superiority.

Such an attitude is mostly seen as arrogant, ignorant, condescending and annoying. It definitely does not help you to find and maintain friends on any level.

**It's not always easy to get along with others**

It is not surprising that it is not always easy to get along with some other people. For thousands of years, humans lived in nomadic groups with enemies all over the place.

Our instinct tells us to defend ourselves, even if it is actually not necessary anymore. Being in any kind of trouble with other humans, it is useful to be aware of that fact.

Psychologists tell us to always, with obvious and proven exceptions, to analyze ourselves before we put blame on others.

- We sometimes have trouble to get along with people without a rational reason
- We are all over-emotional
- Our free will is a wishful thinking
- We are all sometimes hypocrites

**Consider any problem a learning lesson**

This is a perfect opportunity to turn a problem into a learning experience for you and the people you work with.

As intelligent we might consider ourselves, it never hurts to learn something. Wise people claim that you learn more from your problems, mistakes, and failures than you can learn from your success. Think about it.

# The unreasonable idiots

It happens all the time that you meet people who are extremely difficult to get along with, no matter how hard you try. We describe them as crazy or weird. In any case, they are always unreasonable.

Susan Bialy, M.D., described such people and how to deal with them perfectly. As hard as you might try, they never concede and always make you feel bad. In short, they are all the time unreasonable.

- People who twist your words in a non-logical manner to the point when you can't communicate with them anymore
- People who make demeaning comments pretending to be a "joke"
- People who don't respect any boundaries and enjoy annoying you
- People who never accept your point of view and refuse to listen to your argument
- People who behave like bullies
- People who verbally and emotionally abuse other people
- People who intentionally and methodically manipulate other individuals
- People who are straight liars
- People who treat you terribly and generally make you feel bad about yourself
- People who are provocative, unbalanced, and crazy, suggesting there is something wrong with you

- People who are extensively charming but have an ulterior motive for that

**Never wrestle with a pig**

In order to maintain your own peace of mind, you must protect yourself from such toxic personalities.

- Minimize your time with such people as much as you can
- Keep your interaction straightforward and logical
- Don't drink with or around them
- Focus on them in your conversation and volunteer a minimum about you
- Don't ever hope they will change and become better people
- Stay away from hot topics inflaming the conversation even more
- Don't try to convince them about your point of view
- If you absolutely can't avoid spending time with them, create a distraction such as playing with a pet during that time

# The idiots in our own family

Families come in all kinds of variations. Some are picture-perfect, tight-knit families with ideal relationships and built on the premise of nicely working inter-connectedness. Some are not so perfect, causing all kinds of trouble, misunderstandings, and frustration.

The worst kind are toxic families causing a full range of hostilities, battles, and disputes. People from such dysfunctional families usually can't get along at all. They are always fighting, arguing, and wrangling about everything. They hate each other and are sometimes called families from hell.

How can we survive such dysfunctional idiots in our own family? Not an easy task. Many people just turn away and disregard them completely. However, with some family business necessary to be dealt with, this is not always appropriate - or even possible.

Some morons in our own families treat us in a completely unacceptable way. Here a few examples.

- Rejection
- Abandonment
- Neglect
- Abuse
- Manipulation
- Hyper-criticism

If this happens to us, we become automatically more doubtful, fearful, and skeptical. This kind of negative energy leads us into the dark side of life – instead of the bright side of it. This is the worst thing that can happen to you if you ever want to reach your peace of mind.

*(More in my book Find Peace of Mind or Lose Your Mind.)*

**How to protect yourself from a dysfunctional family**

A dysfunctional family relationship virtually always ends up in an emotional and physical health struggle. In order to survive idiots in your own family, you must escape this kind of atmosphere. There are clear signs when you must start acting in order to break out in order to maintain your own sanity.

- Your health and mental well-being starts becoming harmed
- Your emotional, physical, and spiritual status becomes damaged
- Your relationships start to struggle
- You experience some kind of violence, physical or emotional abuse in your life
- You encounter substance abuse such as alcohol or drugs
- You suffer under permanent struggle for power
- You feel necessary distrust and disrespect by your own relatives

You will not survive this kind of wrestling physically, mentally and emotionally if you don't start acting appropriately and on time.

- Acknowledge that idiots will stay idiots. You won't change them
- Sometimes, even during the biggest fight, your best weapon is the kindness
- Get some family counseling
- If you feel you can't take it anymore, move out and find some supporting environment to live.
- Accept that we all have specific limitations of acting and reacting the right way. This also applies to relatives causing trouble and you can't stand.
- Try to stay calm, but also allow yourself to get angry if necessary
- Write a journal and express your feelings on paper
- Do physical exercise in order to diminish your adrenalin level in your body
- Talk to somebody you really trust or find a professional counselor
- Limit your time you must spend with your toxic family in order to minimize your conflicts
- Determine and set-up your emotional and physical health boundaries
- Don't let them be sucked-back into the family feud
- Don't hold grudges. Life is too short for that.

- Learn how to protect yourself with methods such as meditation
- Treat yourself well. Do things that make you feel good and enjoy. Invite friends who love you to join and share your life.
- Try to create a healthy balance in your life such as a healthy diet. Be cautious of compulsive
  behaviors such as over-eating, over-drinking or over-shopping.
- Find peace of mind. (*Access all necessary details in my book "Find peace of mind – or lose your mind. How to survive the collapse of our values, morals, and principles."*)

**The idiotic parents**

Our society introduced us to many behavioral changes, not in compliance with the traditional way of life. First of all, countless "modern" parents don't teach their kids any of the basics of decency, respectfulness, and fairness. The outcome is usually catastrophic.

Millions of kids nowadays don't know the difference between right and wrong. Therefore, they are often totally lost when navigating through societal standards. This doesn't just hurt the parents – but the children too.

Countless young people call their parents "idiots" these days. Many decent actions and reactions any traditional family considers normal and appropriate, millennials simply call stupid, antiquated, and idiotic. Psychologists have some valuable advice for young people who tend to simply brush away their parents and other older people with decades of more life experience than them.

- Try to remain calm
- Try to listen to your parents respectfully
- Explain your position patiently and thoroughly
- Ask parents to do the same
- Acknowledge that you come from different educational backgrounds and perspectives
- Do feel and make sure that you are really able to make own decisions
- Agree to disagree respectfully
- Acknowledge parent's intention to care for you
- Don't ever criticize parents as "out of touch" and old-fashioned
- Try not to feel threatened or wronged
- Don't get upset
- Never say to your parents, "This is none of your business"

**The idiotic grownup children**

Due to a variety of economic, social, and personal reasons, millions of adult children still live with their aging parents. This is causing a number of serious problems on both sides.

Unless there are medical or mental issues at play, major parenting or behavioral mistakes were made and need to be addressed. Countless parents with best intentions in mind make terrible mistakes by "rescuing" their kids from the problems they should solve themselves.

Are you one of these well-meaning but terribly acting parents?

- Are you afraid of saying "no" to your kids?
- Do you sacrifice too much to "help" your kids?
- Are you afraid of "hurting" your child by being strict?
- Does your child like being "entitled" to financial privileges such as car, rent, and gifts?
- Are you "burned out" helping your kids deep into the 20s or 30s?

According to psychologists, the biggest failure while raising children is not to foster independence and not to empower kids.

Don't bail your kids out whenever they face a problem they are supposed to solve themselves! How can children become responsible adults if they never had the opportunity to learn how to solve problems?

Helicopter parents, in their mistaken effort to do the best for their kids, actually accomplish the opposite: a colossal failure! Kids become and stay completely dependent, and many parents even don't know why. This is a catastrophe and a disgrace. It doesn't just ruin
parent's life, but also destroys children's future.

Raising kids responsibly starts at the very beginning. If you missed that point at their early age and your kids
are grown up now, remember this:

- Encourage adult, working children to contribute financially to room and board
- Don't automatically give them money every month. This should always be dependent on children's efforts to gain independence
- Set a time-limit on how long do you accept them to remain home
- If they are in real need, help them with some starting cost renting an own apartment
- Make clear that you always can change your mind about previous commitments
- Be always in full agreement about any kind of financial support
- Set-up limits on how much time and money you want to spend on resolving their crises
- Never forget, you are not in a popularity contest. You have the responsibility of a parent, you are not a "friend" who is supposed to go along all the way. Also, be also prepared

to be rejected. Kid's rejection may change in the near future.

- If your child has any kind of substance abuse problem, join a support group. Giving them money again and again for drugs or alcohol doesn't help them at all. Just the opposite!

## Obnoxious family members

We all hate to admit it, but most of us do have annoying, obnoxious brothers, sisters, cousins, aunts or uncles. We usually can't escape them during the usual family gatherings.

It does not help if you put our head into the sand. We must deal with them. Their annoying attitude kills our mood and makes everybody feel bad. There are many ways how obnoxious people terrorize us.

- Practicing pranks on other people
- Interrupt conversations with their stupid jokes
- Behave like sexist pigs

Psychologists at the University of Arizona analyzed methods how to approach the problem.

- Find out the source of your annoyance. Their actions might not be that bad, but we maybe associate some bad memories and feelings with them. They could be the source of our suffering by inappropriate pranks or jokes.

- Try to ignore the person or their actions completely. When they see that you don't become angry or upset, they see no more purpose in their handling and might stop it by themselves.

- Sometimes, a direct confrontation is the only way to clear the air. Have your facts straight and make your point in a believable, effective communication way.

- Whatever happens, try to preserve everybody's dignity and self-esteem. Always focus on the problem, not the person. You want to win the argument, you don't want to destroy the person!

**Difficult intimate partners**

It is always a burden of dealing with difficult people anywhere and at any time, but this struggle becomes especially unbearable if it involves your intimate partner.

Every close relationship assumes love, respect, caring, and virtually limitless understanding for each other's needs. However, many husbands, wives, or lovers are so self-absorbed that they don't care about you and a sincere relationship at all.

Usually, such a toxic relationship offers only two alternatives: Accepting the unacceptable in order to "save the relationship" – or leaving for good. Both are painful. Unfortunately, there are no good solutions on the table.

If you decide to stay and try to "fix" your problem with the partner you love, psychological research offers some approaches to do just that. Of course, there is no perfect recipe and no guarantee that this would work. Studies, however, have shown that their techniques have some reasonable expectations of success, as Psychology Today reports.

Generally speaking, the approach must include the acknowledgment of each other's feelings and convey the message that you see your lover as a valued partner for life.

Psychologists call this a problem-softening technique. They advise you to try the following:

- Temporarily downplay the problem until the anger and frustration cools down
- Acknowledge each other's efforts to change and improve
- Highlight your partner's positive relationship efforts
- Allow his/her point of view to be discussed
- Hold back with your negative reaction to partner's destructive behavior
- Try to insert your positive energy, feelings, and humor
- Communicate your care and acceptance
- Display optimism about your relationship

Your only chance of success might be the temporary "problem-softening" technique:

- Focus on the good and positive aspects of the relationship
- Reward any kind of positive efforts from the other side
- Redirect any negative developments in a more constructive, positive approach


## The idiotic friends

Life is simple, we just made it complicated. Nothing defines the relationship difficulties better than friendships. We automatically assume that our friends like us for "what and who we are" and because we love them. Sometimes this might be very true. However, the motivations of how, when and why to choose a friend are manifold.

Independent from our emotional affection with people we call friends, we must acknowledge that we have either a genuine - or just a purpose-oriented friendship. Not easy to swallow if you are embedded in a pink cloud.

While we thank God, we still have friends who love us for what and who we are, many of them have a selfish motivation to connect with us. Very often they expect benefits or advantages.

Of course, it can be advantageous to befriend with wealthy people who may own a yacht, a hotel, and a nice vacation home or throw elaborate parties with famous people.

- Often, it's primarily all about the purpose, not necessarily the friendship.
- Some friends may assume sex, others financial rewards, social status, vacation companionship or other egotistical advantages.
- They are using each other just to fulfill a purpose – whatever this may be. Yes, this is social fraud.

Just ask some previously well-situated people who all suddenly went broke, got fired from a lucrative job, or for some other reason lost their money and social status. How many of their "friends" did they keep after the bankruptcy, loss of a job or a prestigious position?

- Check on the status of your friendships
- How often do they call you, when and for what reason?
- Do any of them just contact you if they want something from you?
- Aren't there any friends who virtually never call you, and you emphatically want to keep their friendship by calling them again and again?

Very common also are friendships with people who are always "givers" and others who are constantly just "takers." Some friends are frequently just "using" each other. Nothing is wrong with that if this is okay with you, but be at least aware of it.

**Do you have a toxic friendship?**

Psychologist claim that virtually everybody has friendships they consider toxic. We all wish and hope to have good friends. This is especially true considering our "best" friends.

If we are honest to ourselves, we must admit that many of friendships are sometimes at least uncomfortable. As problematic it may be to admit that some of our friendships are not so perfect as we think, it is advisable to examine our friendly relationships thoroughly.

What are the most obvious warning signs of a toxic friendship?

- Do you find yourself in competition with your best friend?
- Does your best friend spend a lot of talk time with other friends but not with you?
- Are you the one who is always calling and maintaining the friendship?
- Does your best friend have a self-righteous attitude?
- Does your friend tell you that you have to change?
- Are you walking on egg-shells when dealing with your best friend?
- Are you riding an emotional roller-coaster with your best friend at the controls?
- Does your relationship with your best friend stress you out?

Never forget, good, genuine friendships boost your good feeling, positive energy, and immune system. Bad relationships make you sick!

**Don't let them get under your skin**

Unreasonable, stupid, and mean people get easily under our skin. This experience applies especially to our friends who are not always in our corner. Usually, you won't change them, you have to adjust your own attitude towards them.

- Adjust your viewpoint
- Lower your friendship status standards
- Try to imagine their standpoint
- Understand that people are not intellectually equal
- Don't expect them to understand problems they don't know anything about
- Accept that you mostly won't be able to change their mind
- Educate yourself for any dispute you might expect with them
- Avoid keywords and topics controversial to them
- Try to kill them with your kindness
- Don't complain if you can avoid it
- Avoid senseless discussions
- Be patient and stay emotionally balanced
- Use logic with your arguments
- Ask them to clarify their facts and opinions
- Approve their potential strengths
- Don't take anything too personally
- Try to be respectful as much as you can
- Walk away whenever you reach a dead end

**Cherish genuine friendships**

On the other side, never forget how important genuine friendships really are for all of us. How sad and boring would our life be without real, genuine friends?

- Real, good, genuine friendships are among the biggest blessing of our life
- They are never one-sided
- They are always affectionate, reliable and full of love
- They are somehow part of your identity
- We must cherish, treasure and nurse them

- They are like beautiful, sensitive, tender flowers needing our attention whenever necessary
- Don't ever take them for granted
- They are God's blessing

## The idiots at work

For all of us who have to work for a living, our work environment is a very important part of our daily life. In an ideal world, we work in a nice place, have a decent boss, and we get along very well with our colleagues.

Welcome to the real world. A perfect workplace is unfortunately not the rule. Many working people have a terrible jerk as a boss, mean, ultra-competitive and unreasonable co-workers, as well as a general workplace climate making their daily life miserable. Yes, there are workmates and bosses from hell!

Sometimes you meet individuals at work who are utterly ruthless, mean, fearless, and resilient. They are not constrained by any decency or moral code. Sometimes they are smart but very manipulative and hostile to you.

There is no "one recipe fits all" solution. First of all, analyze the situation. Among the questions you have to ask is whether is the person worth worrying about. Maybe the person is so silly that you don't have to waste any energy on it.

In order to find out whether and how condescending your coworkers really are, try to determine what they actually do to you. Here are the clearest signs of trouble ahead.

- They argue with you all the time
- They are tense and sarcastic
- Their body language is disrespectful
- They try to ignore you
- They are laughing at you
- They don't trust you
- They always disagree with you
- They are always defensive
- They never ask you for advice or help
- They never help you
- They mostly avoid you completely
- They never invite you to social gatherings
- They never ask you about your personal life
- They contribute to badmouthing about you
- They are speechless if you succeed
- They steal credit for your ideas

- They pretend unauthorized power.
- They try to throw you under the bus
- They encourage you to leave the company
- You try to impress others at work
- You are irritated and start cursing
- You are horrified for looking dumb
- You are always on your own

It can only get even worse if your boss is an idiot from hell. There are many mean, self-centered, arrogant, ignorant, bullying, and hateful bosses around. According to a poll, about 32 percent of working people complained they have a horrible boss. As tricky it is to deal with them, they are easy to diagnose.

- They lie to you
- They are always right
- They over-promise and under-deliver
- They blame you for everything but never praise you if you succeed
- They expect to think and act just like them
- They micromanage everything
- They call you on a weekend
- They have their favorites, but you are not one of them
- They don't listen to you
- They ignore you
- They want to be always in the center of attention
- They are moody
- They change their mind all the time
- They don't permit you to advance

- They are passive-aggressive

What can you do? Not an easy task if you have to keep your job. If you can't just escape, you have to deal with your boss. You won't change him, so you have to change your attitude towards him and your job.

- Rethink your relationship management
- Utilize all useful flexible work policies of your company
- Start working remotely if possible
- Working from home, a café or a vacation place is not so bad at all
- Watch your emotional stress carefully in order to avoid long-term health problems
- Make a decision at one point whether it is really worth sacrificing so much for your job
- Don't forget that the best job in the world is not worth sacrificing your physical health and personal sanity for it

"Psychology Today" has some very useful advice for people who can't just quit the job in order to escape jerks at work.

**Start with a polite confrontation**

It is sometimes hard to believe, but there are still some people who don't intend to be mean. It does happen that some coworkers are surprised that you feel badly treated by them.

Try to talk to them in a civil manner, and maybe they will admit their wrongdoing and stop being complete assholes.

**Avoid people who are hostile against you as much as possible**

Of course, you must communicate with most of your co-workers all the time, but you surely can minimize the conversations with those who treat you badly.

Instead of meeting them in person, you can sometimes just call them or discuss matters via email. This pretty much keeps some physical and emotional distance between you and the person who dislikes you.

**Turn small wins into big victories**

Whenever appropriate, try to get back to them. Turn your small wins into victories. Fight back! Sometimes they will stop fighting you just because they must anticipate that you don't let them. Don't be a coward!

If, as an example, your coworker steals your food out of the office fridge, put some strong laxative into it next time. Believe me, they won't forget it.

**Detach yourself emotionally from them**

It is very important that you don't let them get under your skin. Since you won't change them, you must change your attitude!

Try not to care what they think, say or do. Try to emotionally disregard them. Try to imagine they don't exist - or at least are of no importance to you.

## Document carefully what they do to you

You never know how the struggle ends. It is always very important to have all the facts straight. This means that you must carefully document all important stages of the match.

Collect all documents proving how they treat you. Copies of your correspondence, such as emails, are very helpful. It is not really rare that the nasty coworkers turn the table on you and start complaining about you at your boss. Every careful documentation can save your butt. Start a diary!

## Assemble fellow victims and witnesses

It is highly probable that the idiotic coworker causing your misery also treats others in a similarly unacceptable way. This is mostly easy to find out.

Talk to other victims and ask them whether they want to join you in fighting the abusive colleague. They will mostly agree with you and join the fight.

At the same time, it is very advisable to collect all witnesses of the obnoxious treatment. Being prepared as much as you can should always be a wise decision to do.

**Consider a legal action as your last resort**

Nobody really likes lawsuits. However, in many situations with no other viable options, they are unavoidable.

There is a growing legal movement against bullying in the workplace. Some law office will even do it on a contingency basis, which means there is no upfront cost to you. You just must share any financial reward with your lawyers.

**Protect your sanity at work**

The main problem at your work is usually not the kind and amount of work you have to manage. Usually, mean, unreasonable, malicious bosses and colleagues cause the aggravation you can't take anymore.
This type of stress and frustration at your work can easily burn you out. This is what you have to avoid under almost any circumstances. There are some general rules on how to deal with this kind of your job problem.

- Maintain a still acceptable stress level all the time. Stress is generally unavoidable and even healthy if you can manage it. It is very important that you relax before any nerve-wrecking event and that you find or create your own "sanctuary" in your company. Also, always stay focused on what is important to you and your work.

- Identify all your workplace challenges and obstacles every day. Do you have enough time, resources, information, and support to accomplish what is expected from you?

- Take advantage of a career support system many employers offer. Spend time with specific advisors, coaches, and mentors available to you. This is particularly beneficial if they are working from outside of your company. In such a case, they are able to provide you the fairest and objective support.

- Maintain an honest conversation with your boss. Don't just focus on the problems you might have with supposedly dumb and idiotic colleagues, propose concrete solutions to any kind of company problems. This would confirm you as a problem solver, not a complainer or trouble maker.

- Preserve all aspects of your personal life. As much as you must sacrifice your time and efforts to the company, never let them take away your privacy and personal peace of mind. *(More in my book "Find Peace of Mind or Lose Your Mind)*

# The idiots in our schools and colleges

Some of the greatest and most dangerous idiots can be found in our educational system. Their fraud and deception are truly mind-boggling.

Except for Marxist sympathizers, nobody really doubts that our educational system presents an unbearable crisis. Exploding cost, failing grades, anti-American and anti-Christian propaganda reveal that the idiots in our schools and colleges are doing terrible damage to our youth and our country. They are true idiots from hell!

Let's analyze the situation first. While our main-stream media rarely criticize our public education system, Conservapedia collected some of the most critical and unacceptable facts:

- 30% of public school students fail to graduate
- 40% of minorities fail to graduate
- 70% of leaving high school unqualified to enter a 4-year college
- 77% of students between 8th and 12th grade use illicit drugs
- 50% of viable public high school teenager pregnancies end in abortions
- 20% of students are involved in dangerous binge drinking
- 10% of our public high schools have a homosexual club
- 10% of students have mental health problems
- 160,000 miss school daily

Public schools in the US employ several million people, spend over four hundred billion dollars per year – this is over 10,000 per student. At the same time, they do the following:

- Censor free speech
- Outlaw classroom prayer
- Outlaw the Bible on campus and refuse any kind of Judeo-Christian values and morals in schools and colleges.

- Promote the Marxist worldview
- Promote a radical environmental agenda
- Promote homosexual indoctrination
- Object to virtually everything that represents traditional American values.

**The idiots brainwashing our kids**

Our educational institutions are in the process of a total "reprogramming" of our children away from morals and values expressed in the Ten Commandments. While gay clubs or Muslim organizations are welcome in many schools, Bible clubs or Pro-Life gatherings are rarely acceptable. What is typical in many US high schools today?

- Banning of the US flag on a school campus.
- Forbidding the Pledge of Allegiance on campus.
- Suspension of students with a Bible found in their school locker.
- Requests for greater "condom availability" in schools are often granted.
- School invitations to gay bars are acceptable.
- Welcoming of all gay, lesbian or transgender ideas on campus.
- Cross-dressing of boys and girls are tolerable
- Labeling Christians as "oppressors."
- Mandatory Arabic classes are increasing.
- Mandatory citing of "Five Pillars of Islam" in the class.
- Mandatory visits and Muslim praying in Mosques.

- Preferential treatment of Muslim and other non-white students.

The total indoctrination of school children with a Marxist worldview is often called "the necessary character education." This is frighteningly like the "re-education" camps communists did in Stalin's Gulags and North Vietnamese, North Korean or Chinese prison camps.

## Our idiots rewriting our history

Progressive educators stopped teaching morality as we did in our Western culture for thousands of years. Not many schools teach American history as the events really happened. They are labeled "oppressive" and "racist." The bias in mandatory schoolbooks rewrote our history to the point of the total denial of our glorious past.

Our free speech, liberty, free market, and personal freedom concept in our Constitution is called "outdated" and "needs a radical revision" in accordance with a Marxist worldview. The Constitution is described as a "living and breathing document" and must be interpreted in accordance with today's Marxist worldview. Why do they undergo such elaborate efforts to brainwash our youth?

"He alone, who owns the youth, gains the future." This is what Adolf Hitler said, breathtakingly identical to what Marxism teaches.

It is no accident that our "National Education Association" propagates Saul Alinsky's communist revolution manual "Rules for Radicals" as required school reading. And there is no accident either that Barack Obama taught Alinsky at the college and also based most of his agenda on it.

**The idiots to watch in our schools**

- Gay and lesbian organizations
- National Education Association
- Planned Parenthood
- SIECUS (Sexuality information and education council of the US)

Legally, their information may brainwash your kids and also put schools in danger of violating constitutional principles and parental rights. The reasons could be because of they:

- Present negative portrayals of some religions and/or give favorable portrayals of other religious or spiritual beliefs.

- Promote school activities that would single out or ostracize religious and/or socially conservative students.

- Politicize the school environment with lobbying campaigns and one-sided messages on political and controversial issues.

- Sexualize classes with one-sided messages promoting homosexuality, bisexuality, transgenderism, etc., while excluding other viewpoints.

## How to fight the idiots in our schools

The advocacy group TrueTolerance.org has published Parents' Bill of Rights protecting your child from political brainwashing and abuse in Marxist-oriented public schools.

- Request and arrange a time to examine textbooks, lesson plans, curriculum and supplemental materials used in their child's classroom.

- Request a time to visit the school and observe their child's classes.

- Meet with teachers, as well as consult with other professionals interacting with their children at school, including counselors, coaches, administrators, etc.

- Inspect their child's school records, including academic, counseling and health information.
- Be notified when medical services are being offered to their child.

- Be notified if the school is aware that their child has been bullied or has been accused of bullying.

- Be notified if criminal action is deemed to have been committed against their child.

- Be notified if their child is accused of a criminal action or an infraction that warrants a significant form of school punishment, such as detention.

- Expect and request an educational environment that is emotionally and physically safe for their children.

- Expect and request an educational environment that respects your child's religious freedoms.

- Be informed of and have the right to appeal to school policies and administrative decisions.

- Receive written notice and the option to opt their child out of surveys that include invasive questions about students' sexual experiences or attractions, their families' beliefs, morality, religion, political affiliations or mental and psychological problems of the student or family members.

- Request a change in class or teacher assignment for their child.

- File a request for information from the school under the Freedom of Information Act.

- Be notified if their child is absented from school or classes.

- Have the opportunity to volunteer or participate on review committees that made decisions about curriculum, lesson plans, and books.

- Receive written notice and have the option to opt their child out of controversial instruction on topics such as sex education, sexual orientation, and homosexuality-related instruction.

- Know which extracurricular clubs and school activities their children are participating in.

**How to fight the idiots in colleges and universities**

David Horowitz Freedom Center developed the "Academic Bill of Rights" Marxists ferociously object to. The reason is that it limits the now virtually unopposed domination of their political activism in our colleges and universities.

- All faculty shall be hired, fired, promoted and granted tenure on the basis of their competence and appropriate knowledge in the field of their expertise and, in the humanities, the social sciences, and the arts, with a view toward fostering a plurality of methodologies and perspectives.

- No faculty shall be hired or fired or denied promotion or tenure on the basis of his or her political or religious beliefs.
- No faculty member will be excluded from tenure, search and hiring committees on the basis of their political or religious beliefs.
- Students must be graded solely on the basis of their reasoned answers and appropriate knowledge of the subjects and disciplines they study, not on the basis of their political or religious beliefs.
- Curricula and reading lists in the humanities and social sciences should reflect the uncertainty and unsettled character of all human knowledge in these areas by providing students with dissenting sources and viewpoints where appropriate. While teachers are and should be free to pursue their own findings and perspectives in presenting their views, they should consider and make their students aware of other viewpoints. Academic disciplines should welcome a diversity of approaches to unsettled questions.
- Exposing students to the spectrum of significant scholarly viewpoints on the subjects examined in their courses is a major responsibility of faculty. Faculty will not use their courses for the purpose of political, ideological, religious or anti-religious indoctrination.

- Selection of speakers, allocation of funds for speaker's programs and other student activities must observe the principles of academic freedom and promote intellectual pluralism.

- An environment conducive to the civil exchange of ideas being an essential component of a free university, the obstruction of invited campus speakers, destruction of campus literature or other efforts to obstruct this exchange will not be tolerated.

- Knowledge advances when individual scholars are left free to reach their own conclusions about which methods, facts, and theories have been validated by research. Academic institutions and professional societies, formed to advance knowledge within an area of research, maintain the integrity of the research process and organize the professional lives of related researchers serve as indispensable venues within which scholars circulate research findings and debate their interpretation.

- To perform these functions adequately, academic institutions and professional societies should maintain a posture of organizational neutrality with respect to the substantive disagreements that divide researchers into questions within, or outside, their fields of inquiry.

Organizations such David Horowitz Freedom Center and TrueTolerance.org offer a wealth of valuable information for freedom and liberty-loving people.

Search for help on how to protect your parental rights. The following progressive advocacy groups flood our schools and colleges with slanted educational material intended in order to promote anti-family viewpoints.

Excellent information also offers excellent non-profit ParentalRightsFoundation.org. Also, the Alliance Defending Freedom points out that you have the following parental rights:

- Choose the school environment that best fits your child's needs, whether public school, charter school, private school, or homeschooling.

- Depending upon where you live, opt your child out of a curriculum that would force them to violate your family's religious beliefs.

- Depending on where you live, review the curriculum and teaching materials for any of your child's classes.

- Opt-out your child from any extracurricular activity.

- Depending upon where you live, be notified if your child is enrolled in a course that includes sex education, family planning, homosexual themes, diversity issues, or extreme violence.

- Access your child's record, including grades, disciplinary, and counseling proceedings.
- Remove your child on days of religious observance.

- Depending on where you live, receive the same tax credits and vouchers to attend religious schools available to attend non-religious schools.

Altogether, we are not completely helpless with the idiots in our schools, colleges, and universities. We just must educate ourselves and take action. There are many traditionally oriented people and organizations who would be happy to help us.

# The idiots in politics

The political absurdity in our life does not seem to know any boundaries. Just a few decades ago, most people would consider all of today's extremely silly political positions as what they really are – stupid, senseless, and straight idiotic.

What do political idiots all over demand or proclaim? Here are just a few most ridiculous, outrageous, and stupid examples.

- Antifa (created as the militant wing of the German Communist Party in the 30s) claiming to fight fascism, while being the most anti-democratic, fascist, and criminal force in the US.
- Black lives matter movement indirectly suggesting that white and other lives don't matter.
- President Trump openly called every name in the book imaginable without any proof.
- Socialism Promotion, even though it has been disproven for hundred years.
- Eliminating poverty through credit cards for everyone
- Eliminating tests in colleges.
- Eliminating grades in colleges.
- Introducing racially segregated buildings in colleges.
- Eliminating male and female gender by defying biology.

- White professors do not need to apply at colleges.
- No more white poets allowed and taught at some colleges.
- Claim that Law enforcement creates micro-aggressions.
- Rep. Steve Scalise shot in Washington.
- Budgeting a Bridge to nowhere in Alaska.
- Comparing ICE to Ku-Klux-Klan (Kamala Harris not knowing that KKK was actually established by the Democratic Party).
- Claim Israel is an apartheid country.
- Claim Islam is a religion of peace.
- YouTube removes Tucker Carlson video for Prager University as "dangerous content."

Even abroad, there is no shortage of stupid political ideas.

- Creation of Beer parties in Canada, the Czech Republic, and Russia.
- Creation of the Wrestler Party in Canada.

**The idiotic political platform**

The Democratic Party used to be a force defending, protecting and promoting the blue-collar people in America. For decades, "Dems" used to be the most popular major power in US politics.

During the last decade, Democrats abandoned their original principles and the most vital foundations of our republic such as the US Constitution.

At the surface, they still commit to the principles of our founding fathers, but in reality, they demand a more "contemporary" (Marxism-oriented) interpretation of the Constitution and Bill of Rights.

They insist that the Constitution can't be interpreted "as written" but as a "living and breathing instrument," allowing all kinds of Marxist-style understandings. Our judges are supposed to "read" a different meaning into the most basic of US laws.

While more and more Democratic politicians openly commit to Socialism, their platform reflects a more and more anti-American, anti-capitalism, and anti-freedom platform. Millions of traditionally oriented people consider this a radical, unreasonable, and anti-democratic, idiotic program.

- Committing to unequivocal abortion right, completely disregarding the protection of human life in mother's womb
- Applauding the same-sex marriage by not acknowledging human traditions and biological facts
- Supporting illegal immigration and suggesting eliminating borders
- Subscribing to global warming and "climate change" despite major fraud in managing scientific data
- Promoting only Government controlled health care system disregarding any kind of individual choice and free-market options

- Strangling the banking and stock market system by over-regulating the entire financial sector
- Endorsing the Iran deal by disregarding its major failures and the high probability of further development of nuclear weapons in Iran
- Approving the Palestinian approach of the Near East problem, totally discounting Israel's vital security concerns
- Insisting on campaign financing benefiting their strategic partnership with Unions
- Fighting any kind of voter ID laws, allowing anybody without a Government ID to be able to vote in order to avoid "voter suppression"

## America is still unique

For over two hundred years, we all considered being "Americans." Unified, under one flag, one Constitution, one national identity.

Contrary to most other countries, America used to be the perfect "melting pot" of different races, ethnicities, and classes. America survived slavery, civil war, both world wars, Jim Crow, and the chaotic sixties. Despite major differences, the process unified US citizens rather than dividing individuals.

The wide-spread identity politics brutally promoted by the socialist left constitutes a series of aspects we must address. As the Hoover Institution points out, our position in the world is absolutely unique:

1. The Declaration of Independence and the American Constitution are unique documents for their time and proved transcendent across time and space. Both documents preserved the idea that all people were created equal and were human first, with inalienable rights from God that were protected by the government.

2. Our two-ocean-buffer made Americas ability to monitor the numbers of new arrivals and the melting pot's ability to assimilate, integrate, and intermarry, immigrants, who would soon relegate their racial, religious, and ethnic affinities to secondary importance.

3. The US is the most individualistic and capitalistic of the Western democracies, blessed with robust economic growth, rich natural resources, and plenty of space. We assumed that our limited government and ethos of entrepreneurialism would create enough widespread prosperity and upward mobility that affluence would create a common bond superseding superficial Old-World ties based on appearance or creed.

In the sixties, America's left start departing from these principles. As the Hoover Institution states, "This shift from the ideal of the melting pot to the triumph of salad-bowl separatism occurred, in part, because the Democratic Party found electoral resonance in big government's generous entitlements and social programs tailored to particular groups.

By then, immigration into the United States had radically shifted. Rather than including states in Europe and the former British Commonwealth, most immigrants were poorer and almost exclusively hailed from the nations of Latin America, Asia, and Africa, resulting in poorer immigrants who, upon arrival, needed more government help."

**Departure from American values**

A half-century later, this change, combined with affirmative action, lead to a huge identity politics and diversity industry instigating millions in government, academia and private sector to depart from American values and start teaching values of other cultures and other countries.

For the major media and the entire Marxist-oriented left, this was the birth of the mushrooming identity politics. They stopped identifying with the American Way of Life and instead started appealing to different ethnic and social groups Democrats saw as their future voter potential:

- Blacks
- Latinos
- Muslims
- Gays
- Lesbians
- Transgenders

This was the end of the American melting pot mindset. If you don't agree with their identity politics agenda, you were called:

- Racist
- Sexist
- Homophobic
- Xenophobic
- Islamophobia

In short, as Hillary Clinton hatefully summarized, a "basket of deplorables". This agenda faces the following facts:

- Racial solidarity of "non-whites"
- Expectations that non-whites share the same attitude. The truth is that Cubans don't get along very well with Mexicans, blacks don't agree with the open-border policies and many social aspects.
- The expected ethnic solidarity could cut in both ways.
- It is uncertain how the immigration flow will develop in the near future.
- Factors such as privilege and class are re-emerging.
- The ideology is eroding the identity politics. One of the reasons is that conservative minority women are not considered "genuine" is because the Marxist ideology supersedes even the leftwing identity politics. Primarily,

it's not about protecting the minority identity. It's only to advance the Marxist ideology.

One of the most disturbing parts of social changes in America is left's political "correctness" which objectively mostly means the opposite of "correct". We all just accepted the description naively not suspecting the reason and long-term political effect. Why do we still do that?

In order to reach the Marxist objective, the proponents had to change our logical, objective and traditional descriptions to "politically correct" (Marxist-style) language. This is broadly brainwashing not just our children - but also the entire society.

Wide sections of the Democratic Party nowadays fully subscribe to Saul Alinsky's Rules for Radicals. Their main modus operandi are methods you could in the past only find in the toolbox of communist revolutionaries:

- Attack
- Defame
- Destroy

The majority of our media outlets are more than happy to join their fight against the American Way of Life, free market, free speech, and individualism. As idiotic as it is, collectivism is the preferred objective of the left anywhere.

Wherever Democrats stand in stiff competition with their opponents, all hell breaks loose. All fighting methods are permitted – as long as this promotes their Marxist cause and destroys the enemy. The end always justifies the means.

Empty accusations with no proof at all, such as in the case of Justice Kavanaugh, happen on the daily basis against President Trump and his supporters. Democrats even try to destroy companies with conservative business philosophy.

California Democratic Party initiated a boycott and efforts for the destruction of the In-N-Out burger chain, a very successful Christian company. What was supposed to be their "crime"? They just donated $25,000 to the Republican Party. For Democrats, this is enough to be put on the list the companies slated for destruction.

**Political correctness**

Political correctness is the word of the year. It automatically assumes that all Constitution-based, conservative, traditional family values are "politically incorrect" and therefore must be unequivocally transformed into a politically correct narrative. This description is always based on their Marxist worldview. What does the PC police specifically want?

- Elitism: They pretend to be morally superior to conservatives

- Futurism: They pretend to predict the future better than our experienced-based judgment
- Collectivism: Individuals don't matter, the socialist-style collective must be preferred for a "better good" of the society
- People control: Their Marxist worldview measures are supposed to control everything from your birth until your death

The main anti-American and anti-democratic political correctness demands by the idiots from hell are:

- Do not favor any ethnic group over another
- Do not infringe on any groups sovereignty
- Do not interfere with any minority group
- Do not hinder society to protect specific cultural groups
- Do not promote any ethnic or cultural "stereotypes"

# The idiots in our culture

Our "American Dream" is deeply broken. America's popular culture departed from virtually everything we value and cherish by sticking to our traditional way of life.

Nothing is the way it used to be anymore. All aspects of our lives have changed dramatically. Lies and deception surround us from all corners of our daily life.
What we might not suspect is that we have changed also. We may be lying to ourselves, and we just don't realize it yet.

- The culture shapes our perceptions by telling is what is appropriate, offensive or provocative
- The culture influences our behavior by setting standards about how we communicate with each other
- The culture shapes our personalities by suggesting to us all to either prefer individualism or collectivism

What happened to our culture? Who is responsible? There many reasons why our way of life in many ways already deteriorated to a gutter culture. Yes, it is our dwindling culture. The pop culture in particular.

Most of the pop culture "stars" live in an alternate reality we have nothing in common with. It's pretty much like a weird, brutal, selfish horror movie. We are trying to escape, but there appears to be no way to get out of it.

## Hollywood-style maniacs dominate our culture

These Hollywood-style, egocentric maniacs are overtaking our culture, morals, values, and beliefs. There are no more decency standards, no more honor, no more truth, no more fairness, no more respect.

Everything goes, mostly exactly in accordance with the Marxist worldview. *(Find more information about different worldviews in my book "Find Peace of Mind – or Lose Your Mind. How to survive the collapse of our values, morals, and principles")*

The behaviors of our pop culture personalities are unbearably extreme.

- Narcissistic
- Psychotically self-confident
- Attention-deficient
- Fame obsessed

There is no shortage of pop culture superstars, Hollywood elites, and other egomaniacs who are trashing traditional Americans and destroying our dear American Way of Life. Here are just some of their most idiotic and totally unrealistic ideas.

- Anything goes if it "feels good" and fulfills their narcissistic purpose
- There is no more good or bad, just "different"
- Free healthcare for everyone
- Free monthly income for everyone
- Job guarantee for everyone
- Free college for everyone
- Federal jobs can't include military or law enforcement
- Eliminate the Supreme Court
- Eliminate the Electoral College
- Abolish all borders and ICE
- Introduce a community-led policing nationwide
- Delete all conviction record for felons
- Guarantee free public transportation for everyone

This all did not happen overnight but very gradually when our sub-consciousness no longer could determine between truth and lies, deception and honesty. Our perception of things has changed. The phenomenon is very common when we are bombarded with lies and dishonesty and can't see the difference anymore.

As dictators like Hitler and Stalin pointed out, you start believing any falsehood if it is repeated often enough. Sometimes politicians are lying, our bosses or colleagues are lying, our business or personal partners are lying, our advertising is lying. There is no wonder that we often start believing the falsehoods.

**The poison of the falsehood**

One of our worst enemies is the poisonous effect of falsehood – wherever it comes from. We must identify it and correct our perception. In our daily life, often it doesn't matter so much what the actual truth is, but what our perception of the truth is. The reason is that we don't make our judgments on the "complete truth and nothing but the truth" but through our perception; doesn't matter how wrong the facts may be.

It is somehow like the basics of communication theory. It doesn't matter what you say, it only matters what people hear or assume to hear. We must start being aware that people talk a lot, but how much of it is true or at least in some way correct? Very often not talking or (even better) not listening is the smartest way to go.

Some of our major problems are:

- The majority of our public is badly or not informed at all about the most important matters of our life. They are called "low information" people who get their knowledge from occasional headlines, at best. These headlines usually offer no information or explanation and are virtually always highly deceiving.

- Most people make all their decision emotionally. Facts don't matter. Therefore, politicians, as well as regular people, make nowadays more stupid and unreasonable than ever because they are just based on their "feelings."

- Our culture demands that everything must be done instantly. There is no patience for anything or anybody. We have the urge to buy everything, decide everything, act on everything "right now." This mostly causes major problems.

- Most personal, political, or media discussions only scratch the surface of the problems. Rarely, if ever, the reporters really explain the problem and show what or who is really behind it.

**Even smart people make stupid choices**

We automatically imply that smart, highly educated people make smart, reasonable choices. This is only partially correct. How can smart people defy reasonable logic?

First of all, smart people too fall prey to lies and deception. Then, being perceived as educated, they insist on always being right and have difficulties admitting a mistake or falsehood. This is especially the case with young, inexperienced but highly educated people who build an ego around their personality and strongly defend their "righteousness."

All too infrequently they face someone who is tenacious enough to dissect their failing logic. Sometimes a new boss, colleague, friend or spouse can do that. For them, it is much "easier" to change their job, friends or even spouse than to admit how wrong they are. It culminates at a point when they are deeply convinced that their "version of truth" is actual truth. This kind of untruthfulness is hardest to detect and dismantle. Logical thinkers are rare, and people that admit their mistakes even more.

**Dangers of collective thinking**

Very common but highly dangerous is the kind of group thinking sociologist call "communal thinking". In most areas of life, it seems pleasant to share "collective" ideas as a way of processing information. Any kind of peer pressure affects our intellect very negatively.

All people who become "social animals" have lost their individuality and think, behave and act like ants. This automatically narrows their view of things and their capability to act rationally, creatively and be an independent mind.

Focus groups prove that group thinking does not offer much of diversity in thought and dealing with different ideas. This is typical for political parties and especially activist groups who insist on a "collective opinion" and no individual departure from it is tolerated. The Democratic Party currently does not accept any deviation of their ideology and talking points.

If you belong to such a group, you should try to socialize with people who don't automatically agree with you and who might challenge your opinions. Don't ever follow "smart" people if they are group thinkers (such as radical environmentalists or followers of the totally unverified evolution theory). Sometimes they don't act very smart at all. They often:

- Follow stupid ideas
- Blindly follow stupid ideologies
- Act stupidly because they are angry
- Are trained and educated to act stupidly
- Inherit bad ideas from their parents
- Just want their wrongs to be true

It is sometimes extremely difficult to identify a broad deception because most people believe what you believe and don't know what is genuine and what is deception.

Be very careful of statements such as "most scientists believe that…". A "majority opinion" does not necessarily express anything about the truth. It just means that the majority believes it.

The majority opinion is just an opinion – not a scientific fact! Therefore, don't rely on others too much. They could be victims of the same societal deception as you are.

## Cultural indicators

Nothing happens without reason. Since so much has changed dramatically during the last decades, let's search for some of the factors what else changed dramatically during the same time.

Dr. Chuck Missler summarized the leading cultural indicators over the last three decades. Statistically, the population grew about 41%, the gross domestic product rose 300%, and social spending skyrocketed to 500%. And what is the result of this?

During the same time, the following catastrophic changes happened:

- Violent crime exploded 560%
- The number of illegitimate births went up 400%
- The divorce rate increased by 400%
- Single-parent homes tripled to 300%
- Teenage suicides increased 200%
- SAT scores went down 75%

Why? This does not make any logical sense, does it? For a very specific reason, since 1963 the following cultural and social changes started to be more and more evident:

Never before, have we experienced an escalation of divorce rates, family breakups, homosexuality, teenage pregnancies, illegal drug use, the murder of unborn babies – and virtually all aspects of crime.

What happened in 1963 that changed in America and put our social and cultural structure so much upside down?

You guessed it. The Bible was outlawed in all American schools!

This legal maneuver by Marxism-oriented atheists pushed by the ACLU (some people ironically call American Communist Lawyers Union) destroyed the very basic structure of American Way of Life, founded on Christian values, morals, and principles. There was no more room for the Bible or the Ten Commandments, the backbone of our society and the Judeo-Christian Western civilization.

**No more Ten Commandments**

This was probably not the only reason for the suicidal downfall of our culture, virtually everything we believed in. Even though our Constitution and our Bill of Rights with freedom of speech, freedom of religion, pursuit of happiness still are legally binding, the total removal of the Bible and the Ten Commandments from schools and public space reduces our education to nothing more than force-fed paganism on our children, including the biggest fraud in human history: the evolution theory.

What happens if there are no more values, morals, and principles as described in the Ten Commandments?

What exactly are we are experiencing now?

- Despair
- Confusion
- Depression
- Lack of ideals
- Lack of spiritual and moral values we can believe in

We got what we bargained for. We let the Marxist idiots from hell take over America, over our values, morals, and principles. They are laughing about us how easy it is to fool, deceive, and destroy our culture and our way of life. As naïve as we are, we let it happen.

**Why is the culture so important?**

What is culture? The word basically refers to the pattern of human activity and the symbols representing our life structure. It is represented through the art, literature, costumes, customs, and traditions of an entire community.

Our culture is our national identity.

We can find very distinctive cultures in different parts of the world. The regions and their natural environment greatly affect the lifestyle of the people in that region, shaping their culture.

The multiplicity in the cultures around the world is also a result of the mindset of the people living in different regions of the world.

The culture is a perfect bond that ties the people of a region or community together. It is the most important common bond, which brings the people of a community together.

All customs and traditions that the people of a community follow, the holidays they celebrate, the kind of clothing they wear, the food they eat, and most importantly, the cultural morals and values they adhere to, bind them strongly together.

As sociologists point out, the cultural values help to develop a sense of belonging, and a feeling of unity in the minds of the people of that particular culture.

People of each culture share their traditions and also mostly their ideologies. Members of a particular culture have a similar way of thinking and living.

If they even belong to the same religion, their belief system is the same, this especially leads to a feeling of unity among them.

Nobody really disputes the importance of a culture for a nation. Most people have a natural instinct to preserve and protect their culture. Therefore, all traditionally oriented people are against "watering down" their cultural identity. The following aspects of our national character and identity bind us together.

- Our ancestry
- Our self-realization
- Our history
- Our religion
- Our moral values
- Our knowledge
- Our compassion
- Our meaning of life
- Our safeguard for future generations
- Our responsibility to preserve our culture for future generations

Social sciences view the culture as a part of civil rights and human ethics. They encompass virtually our entire life.

- Freedom of expression
- Right to cultural heritage
- Right to practice all aspects of a culture
- Right to protect the intellectual and material benefits
- Right to participate in cultural life
- Right to choose a ones-own culture
- Right to the protection and development of a culture
- Respect for cultural identity and protection

Every culture has a major socio-economic impact for all people involved and is always a major factor in forming our daily life.

- Propounding the cultural bond and integration
- Influencing innovation and creativity
- Determining individual vs. collective educational alternatives
- Prompting healthcare options
- Shaping economic opportunities
- Defining the society and its social behavior

## Idiotic sitcoms and reality TV dumbing us down

Does watching TV makes us stupid? Yes and no. If you watch selectively and focus on serious informational, good entertainment, and inspirational programming, it may make us smarter.

If you, however, keep watching the low-end trash TV, don't expect to ever escape the dumbing-down effect on you.

Our culture is what we do or not do, what we think or not think, how we act, react, and behave. There is nothing more typical for our mass culture than our popular sitcoms.

Even if you don't watch the low-life-style sitcoms or reality shows on TV, you can't escape their influence on the print and other media. Viewing Kim

Kardashian's behind on CNN.com, some people are getting uncomfortable. Is this what our daily life is all about? Entertainment, celebrities, subculture.

Instead of following this type of idiotic culture, shouldn't we rather do something better?

- Reading a book
- Learn something
- Stop buying their junk

**Most ridiculous student demands**

Most colleges and universities in the Western world are nowadays pure breeding grounds for Marxists and naïve, silly fools with no connection to the reality at all. Forbes documented some of the most ridiculous college protests and demands we've seen so far.

- Amherst students, called "Amherst Uprising," objected to "oppression" on the campus caused by free-speech supporters. They demanded that the free speech fans to be disciplined and "be required to attend extensive training for racial and cultural competency."

- Yale students demanded Halloween costume guidelines. A professor who dared to question university's "Intercultural Affairs Committee" and does not teach there anymore.

- Oberlin College students complained that their cafeteria's food isn't diverse enough. The food "has a history of blurring the line between culinary diversity and cultural appropriation by modifying the recipes without respect for certain Asian countries' cuisines."

- University of Texas Austin students protested the concealed carry permits with dildos. Students were "strapping gigantic swinging dildos to their backpacks in protest of campus carry."

- Brown University students stage a "Die-in" by protesting the "occupation of America" with our Columbus Day.

- Siena College students protested kitchen renovation advertisement as "sexist." This supposedly promotes the "patriarchy."

- Williams College students declared the "Uncomfortable Learning series" with a conservative feminist as much "too uncomfortable" to tolerate and to accept.

- Across America, students march for "free College" in our country. They demand tuition-free colleges, cancellation of all student loan debt, and a minimum wage of $15 for all. No suggestions though how to pay for the multi-trillion-dollar tab.

- California Polytechnic University students organized a "Shit-in" in order to protest the lack of "gender-neutral" bathrooms. Students were encouraged to sign a mock toilet during the protest, on which messages such as "poop equality" signs were posted.

- UC San Diego students arranged a "Free the Nipple" event in order to protest gender inequality. They demanded to "normalize the female breast" by walking topless. Strangely, the girls still covered their nipples.

## The idiots in our media

Unfortunately, idiots are present in every aspect of our life. The worst and most harmful ones are hundreds of media outlets trashing us, the Western civilization, Christianity, Constitution, and free-market society on a daily basis.

All traditionally oriented Americans feel offended how terribly bias about 90% of the US media organizations are. Most journalists are ideologically Democrats and deny their political affiliation with left-wing causes.

Surveys over the last fifty years confirm, however, that journalists are on average much more "Marxist" than the rest of the country. This applies particularly to media people in leading positions.

It is common knowledge and taught in the first semester of every Journalism school that news reporting shall be strictly divided in "news" (fact-based report about specific events) and "commentary" (opinion).

Nobody objects to personal opinions in a newspaper or on TV, but for hundreds of years, they were separated from the news and specifically marked as opinion, commentary or personal view. We still have "opinion pages" and "opinion commentaries" everywhere, and nobody objects to that.

## Media research proves a blatant dishonesty

The trust in most of our media organizations is at the lowest level ever. This did not happen by accident. Everybody experiences media bluffs every day. The sad part is that most cases of "incorrect reporting" are not "innocent mistakes" but carefully executed manipulations of the news content.

We can't avoid the impression that the media bias is a systemic problem. The criticism and negative spin on virtually all traditional points of view are practically never individual. It almost always appears to be "coordinated" throughout the media outlets with the Marxist worldview.

Who is coordinating this "organized" approach against the conservative people and views? Incidentally, many of the topics and spins word by word reflect the talking points of organizations like "Media Matters" and other leftist combat squads financed by the communist billionaire George Soros.

In short, ABC, CBS, NBC, MSNBC, CNN, New York Times, and Washington Post stories against Bush, Trump or Christians are virtually identical. Does this happen by accident?

According to media research, there are different types of media lies and distortions we face every day.

- Patterns of invented and practically always unfounded assumptions and uncorrected errors in news reporting that always support the Marxist worldview.

- News manipulation by omission is the most common practice in newsrooms nowadays. They just "omit" all news stories not complying with their ideology. Therefore, positive stories about conservative movements or people just don't reach the level of newsworthiness. Thousands of scientists who are skeptical about global warming never get any news coverage.

- News bias by selection is another daily method of "selecting" only topics benefiting their leftist worldview. As an example, global warming alarmist always gets great exposure. There hasn't probably been any magazine without a series of praising cover stories on Michelle Obama. On the other side, have you ever seen one cover story with Melania Trump, who speaks five languages and used to be a top international fashion model?

- The manipulation by news placement at the top of the newspaper cover page is also a very common way to promote news with leftist worldview versus conservative stories.

- The selection of "experts" who always just represent their ideology is a daily practice at most news outlets. Have you ever seen expert interviews on CNN not reflecting their own bias?

- The spin method too is a daily tool for fooling the audience. The political activists playing "journalists" focus endlessly on meaningless aspects of events, while the major aspects are completely avoided.

- The labeling of political organizations and ideas with negative, stigmatizing expressions such as "far right," "extremists," "ultra-conservative" happens every day. At the same time, Marxists are labeled as "liberals," "mainstream," and "moderates."

- News manipulation by policy preference and recommendation can be observed every day also. Example: Obamacare got, despite blatant failures, the widest praise in US media. The free-market-oriented, individual choice type of health insurance alternative barely was mentioned in the media at all.

**Mind manipulation and manufactured stories**

Most people are not aware the news they consume are mostly not "news" at all but manufactured stories with the purpose to manipulate our mind.

The majority of the news we consume through the so-called main-stream-media is not primarily produced to inform us objectively. It is often just propaganda intended to fool us and tell us lies.

As the Wakeup-World describes, propaganda is the act of deliberately spreading false or deceptive information, ideas, rumors, doctrines or principles propagated by an organization or movement to help or harm a target person, group of people, movement, institution, nation, etc.

In our daily life, it's the purposeful distortion of information to suit a particular agenda. "Along with its 'proper' use comes the ability to control the masses and mold the collective mind".

**Idiots, liars, and journalists**

There is not one single day in America without major lies, deceptions, and manipulations in our media. The sad truth is, however, that two-thirds of people don't follow any kind of news - or maybe just glance of the headlines. They are completely clueless, and they behave and vote accordingly.

Therefore, the evil media activists find easy prey because the majority does not recognize the manipulation - or does not care. In short, they consider us stupid enough not to comprehend the daily deceit.

- How can New York Times use a moral equivalence of Hamas and Israeli Defense Forces and never explain the real cause for the Gaza violence?

- How can YouTube describe Tucker Carlson's Prager University video as "dangerous content"?

- How can media not ask who organized and paid for the caravan of illegals from Central America?

- How can our news outlets disregard the fact that Google actively supports the communist Chinese Government exercising censorship and tracking its own citizens?

- How come that millions of viewers don't object that MSNBC and other news organizations only allow one viewpoint?

- How come that Marxist worldviews are always described as "mainstream" and "moderate," while traditional, Christian viewpoints are mostly labeled as "controversial" or "far-right"?

- How come that virtually all "mainstream" media companies regularly omit major news facts if they don't fit their narrative?

- How come that we repeatedly read headlines such as "Israelis shot a Palestinian boy" and ignore the fact that the boy attacked Israelis first and they just acted in defense?

- How come that terror attacks by Muslims are always under-reported, while any kind of violence by Americans are mostly blown out of proportion?

- How come that there is virtually no news coverage of the Christian genocide in the Middle East?

- How come that our TV Networks spent fifteen times more air time on the White House

Correspondent's dinner than on the entire Benghazi scandal?

- How come that our media outlets treat the violent Antifa (founded as a military wing of the German Communist Party in the 30s) as a "free speech" and a "peaceful protest"?

- How come that our media apply the constitutional due process only to themselves and other left-wingers - but not to Republicans?

**The "whores" of our free speech**

It happens all over again every day. The stories we read, watch or hear are usually just partially true at best. Mostly they are totally twisted – or completely wrong.

Our indispensable right to a free speech unfortunately also fosters bad guys with a terrible intent who take advantage of our freedom-loving laws. Therefore, countless news stories we consume only serve the one-world elite.

Such propaganda is nowadays called public relations. PR purposely manufactures content and is sometimes called the "whore" of the free speech.

As if this wouldn't be bad enough, we are not just being lied to by our mainstream media. Some of the biggest news manipulations happen when they ignore some of the most important stories of the day.

One weekend in November 2018, eight Israelis were killed and 108 badly injured by over 200 Palestinian rockets. No mention in US and European media. When Israelis counter-attacked and one Palestinian got hurt, however, most of the media outlets produced big stories about the "Israeli aggression" against the Palestinians.

**The propaganda wars**

What is particularly despicable is that many journalists mix personal views and comments with strict "neutral" news reporting and, even worse, even denying it. Unfortunately, this is our daily reality.

All so-called "mainstream media", which are actually by far not "mainstream" anymore, follow just their own political agenda. They claim to be journalists, but they are nothing more than political activists. "American Journalism is dead," a popular Fox News anchor Sean Hannity said for years - and millions of Americans agree.

Everybody wants journalists to be "objective" and keep their personal opinions private. However, everybody also knows that this is just a theory. The Media Research Center (MRC) has accomplished excellent work in documenting America's media reality. Here are just a few examples.

- Spinning election midterms
- Burying six democratic scandals in one year
- Trump's economic success totally ignored
- Same playbook used for Justice Kavanaugh they practiced on Justice Clarence Thomas
- Obsessed with "Russian election interference"
- Disregarded the fact that Google helped Hillary

## Idiots on the web

If you think just our friends, colleagues, teachers, bosses, and journalists are crazy, you haven't seen anything yet. Take a look at the information and entertainment jungle on the Internet!

Yes, it is a good thing that we still have some kind of freedom of speech online. At the same time, this freedom of expression is terribly misused all over the planet every day.

We really have a major dilemma. On the one side, we must protect the freedom of Internet expression under all circumstances. At the same time, millions of people put unbearable junk online all the time.

Governments and other power-hungry forces pretend to "protect" us from uncomfortable information online and call it "hate speech." The central question is who determines what is "hate speech"?

In several European countries, hate speech is criticizing Islam, but not Christianity. How come?

Unfortunately, we have to fight a war on two fronts. We must insist that any kind of free speech includes expressions making somebody uncomfortable. Rightful criticism is free speech, doesn't matter how "offended" some people are.

In the same breath, we must fight lies, deceptions, and manipulations online whenever we encounter them. However, this can't be through legal or Government regulations. They always go overboard and do more harm than good!

There are some tips on how to deal with unreasonable people online.

- Disemvowel your text by using Firefox disemvowel tool
- Temporarily disable comments on a post
- Allow discussions only by email
- Never post any personal information online

- Let everything cool off by doing nothing
- Bailout when still is time
- Prove your argument whenever possible
- Always let the idiots have the last word

## Social media: Best and worst at the same time

Social media sites still guarantee the easiest way of free expression for us, average people. The misuse of the opportunity has, however, devalued the system in a way that makes it difficult to swallow.

Social media represents the best of free speech – and the worst of misuse and manipulation. It is like a box of very best chocolate candies and the worst of despicable garbage at the same time.

Most idiots of any kind can be easily found on the social media, which is especially harmful to young people who are addicted to it. What does it to us?

- Promotes anxiety and depression
- Allows cyber-bullying
- Instigates the fear of missing out
- Stimulate unrealistic expectations
- Overstate body-image
- Causes unhealthy sleep-patterns
- Leads to addiction
- Encourages an unlimited distribution of party pictures.
- Ensures the comparison with others
- Promotes oversexualized behavior and clothing
- Fosters viral video escapades

- Supports public humiliation and shaming
- Stimulates shallow friendships
- Sponsors isolation
- Leads to wasting valuable time

## How to maintain our sanity despite idiots

Our conventional approach to viewing the world and to comprehend the events and societal changes does not work anymore.

The reason is that the Marxism-infected left destroyed our common sense, logic, rational reasoning and civilized discussion about aspects that matter most in our life.

They exchanged it with a radical agenda terribly hurting all people who want to follow a peaceful, traditional, conservative way of life.

**Discover who your enemies are**

This destructive radicalism has reached a point where a normal discourse is virtually impossible. A normal democratic "political fight" has been replaced by name-calling, personal destruction, and street violence – just as "Rules for Radicals" by communist propagandist and Obama idol Saul Alinsky demand.

What can we do? We seem to be doomed if we capitulate. We feel doomed if we fight back. The only chance we have is, to change the game, to think outside of the box.

By finding new perspectives and approaches we won't change the world, but we might find our peace of mind.

**Think outside of the box**

Does your goldfish inside his bowl know how life outside of the bowl is?

This is a much too simplified example, but it still visually demonstrates the problem. Inside of our nicely warm or comfortably air-conditioned home, we can't really feel how cold or hot it is outside.

Our mind does not really work very much differently. Our consciousness and subconsciousness don't like to be forced outside of our "comfort zone" and want to stay inside the box.

You must "force" them out, just like expecting your kids not to become couch potatoes but to get out and get some fresh air. Outside of the box thinking is pretty much like "fresh air" - versus the sticky, inside atmosphere.

**Think positively**

Negative thoughts are killing our day. Let's try to avoid them at almost any cost. If you reach a positive attitude, you will be happier, healthier, more successful, well balanced and even more popular. All efforts to become positive are worth the trouble or inconvenience.

Learning how to get a positive attitude is fun. Below are some of the most promising "rules" you must adhere to if you want to start thinking positive.

Have you paid attention to the fact that your day heavily depends on how you started your day? If you are late and start panicking, negative emotions and a pessimistic view will often carry you through the day. You feel nothing good can happen during the rest of the day.

On the other hand, if you start your day with a positive attitude, letting positive thinking dominate you, the rest of the day will be mostly positive, too. If you are in doubt, look in your mirror in the morning and say to yourself, "Today will be a good day". Your attitude will change.

It is inevitable that you encounter obstacles, negative experiences or hurdles during your day at home or work. There is no such thing as a flawlessly "perfect day". Get used to that, but filter out the bad aspects such as "stuck in the traffic" and try to siphon a positive aspect out of this situation. Example: Now I finally have enough time to listen to my favorite radio station or think through something I didn't have time to before.

**Find humor in your life**

The happiest and most popular people are the ones who find a humorous aspect in almost anything. You might remember how some funny people tell jokes at a party. They can laugh about themselves and their stupidity when they mention something that happened on their last vacation. For example, somebody forgot the sunscreen and got a bad sunburn all over the body and still describes the event humorously:" When I was a kid I always wanted to look red like an Indian. Now I finally got my wish…"

**Don't get dragged into other people's fights**

Life is complicated enough. Don't let other people drag you into their problems, fights or complaints. Don't fall into the trap of negativity, bad mood, and negative energy. Never forget the saying: "It's not my cup of tea."

Negative situations, even if they are not yours, take you down, make you angry, sad and maybe even aggressive. Only a positive attitude leads you to your badly needed peace of mind.

**Smile and make other people smile**

Let people see you smile often. Smiling will automatically promote your "feel good" attitude. Everybody knows that happy people always smile, but only very few are aware that this system also works the other way around. Medical tests have shown that even a short period of smiling actively releases a "happy hormone" and physically improves your mood.

**Manage your stress**

Positive stress is good, negative stress is terrible for your attitude and your health. Medical researchers confirm that optimism has substantial benefits to your health:

- Longer life
- Less depression
- Less exhaustion
- Better immune system
- Better resistance to the common cold
- Better psychological status
- Better physical status
- Better cardiovascular system
- Better prepared to manage hardships and stress

**Be an optimist**

You can easily find out whether you are an optimist or pessimist. Check out whether you are an optimist or pessimist.

If you agree to that you are a pessimist, don't worry. You can learn how to be positive. See how optimists deal with the same challenges:

- This is an opportunity to learn something new
- I'll try it from a different angle
- Necessity is the mother of inventions
- It didn't fit into my daily schedule, but I am going to re-examine this
- I can try to make it work
- Let's take a chance
- I'll try to open some new channels of communication

- I'll give it another try

Under the very same challenges and circumstances, pessimists and optimists produce very different outcomes. Never forget, everything is attitude! Hopefully, you'll find a positive one.

**Learn patience**

Impatience is part of our instant-gratification society, which is a major problem not many people can really manage. It leads to terrible frustrations, bad mood, and unhappiness. Why? It's because we want everything "right now", instantly.

Millions of people are happy to pay unreasonable overnight shipping fees just because they immediately want to be in possession of virtually meaningless items they bought online. There is no rationality in their actions, just raw, pure, senseless emotion.

We all must learn patience. How? There is no "wonder pill" or "one-size-fits-all" solution, but there are valuable tips you might want to try.

- Find out why you are impatient
- Determine what triggers your impatience
- Why are most of your decisions emotional and follow the "collective" mass trends instead of individualism? Write down your reasoning
- Investigate how impatience hurts your mind and body
- Get rid of unnecessary things
- Remember what really matters in your life
- Find out how to change your behavior
- Step back with your emotions

- Exercise gratitude
- Fight instant gratification by making yourself wait
- Practice uncomfortable things
- Take some deep breaths
- Begin to transform impatience into patience

Patience is a skill we are not born with, we must learn and experience it. We all can develop more patience if we don't want to be like a hungry, red-faced, shrieking baby impatiently expecting instant satisfaction.

Just sit down at your piano and play a peaceful song. Don't ever be impatient or angry with yourself just because you might not be perfect.

Our "urgency" in expecting or doing things instantly is a natural defense mechanism to protect ourselves. In ancient times, this was an important skill. Nowadays, it's not necessary and is more harmful than helpful. Impatience can become an addiction.

You may not be aware that the opposite of "patience" is irritation, anger, blame, shaming and other highly negative and dangerous conditions we must confront to solve our impatience problems.

We always want to be comfortable in all situations, but this does not reflect the real world. Some people are surprised that we must learn to accept discomfort, too.

Distress, awkwardness, and even pain have a very specific purpose in our lives. They "push" us into finding solutions we are endlessly postponing or are not aware of.

## The idiots and the lessons we've learned

Dealing with dumb, mean, and obnoxious people is hard. There is no general recipe how to react to them or how to treat them.

First of all, don't let them ruin your day and suck you into a mud fight.

Don't wrestle with pigs! The jerks probably enjoy it, but this is a fight you can't win, at least not at a somehow civilized level.

At the same time, you can't give up. A few life lessons might help to protect yourself from harming your body, mind, and soul. There is some psychological advice you should never forget.

- Idiots will be idiots
- Interact with them at a distance
- Be kind to everybody
- Laugh it off
- Silence is often the best response to idiots
- Protect your energy
- Be yourself
- Meditate if you can
- Don't care what others think
- Don't let others define you
- Know that others have the same kind of problems
- Don't try to "fit in" at any price
- Don't be judgmental
- Don't stay in bad relationships
- Never make life decisions in a hurry and anger
- Enjoy life

**A positive approach to negative people**

Interacting with nasty people full of negative energy is very stressful. We always want to avoid it if in any way possible. However, mostly we don't have a choice, and we must respond appropriately.

But what is appropriate? We don't enter a big fight, but we don't want to give up either. If you have peace of mind, use your positive attitude to solve the problem on your terms.

- Stay calm
- Separate the person from the issue
- Reduce unnecessary frictions
- Focus on positive aspects of the relation
- Focus on aspects of the interaction you can control
- Shift from reacting to being proactive
- Change from following to leading the dispute
- Kill them with kindness
- Breathe mindfully
- Use an app for conflict management
- You pick the battle if necessary
- Put the spotlight on them
- Call them out
- Zig when they zag
- Confront bullies
- Don't scream, yell, and push
- Don't get caught in a fight you don't want

Set your own boundaries

- Keep enemies close to your chest
- Let them vent
- Try to be a part of the solution – not the problem
- Explain the consequences
- Be professional
- Be honest and faithful to yourself
- Use appropriate humor

- Laugh about it

If you have a choice, considering all aspects important to you, ask yourself whether it's worth dealing with idiots. Usually, the anger, frustration, and wastefulness of time and energy aren't worth interacting with unreasonable, mean, and hostile people.

If you have any options left, don't wrestle with pigs!

*"Never argue with an idiot. They will drag you down to their level and beat you with experience."*
*(Mark Twain)*

**References**

- Media Research Center

- Reasons.org

- Prager University

- Psychology Today

- Find Peace of Mind or Lose Your Mind
- by Pierre A. Kandorfer, Ph.D.

- No More Doubt – Science Confirms the Bible
- by Pierre A. Kandorfer, Ph.D.

- Fight Back Manual – Last Bet Strategies for Survival of Western Civilization
- by Pierre A. Kandorfer, Ph.D.

- Liberals Hijacking America – A satirical Eye-Opener
- By Pierre A. Kandorfer, Ph.D.

## Books by Pierre A. Kandorfer:

- Good, Kind, and Happy
- 
- You Don't Know Who You Are

- End Game – When truth doesn't matter anymore

- Whom Can We Still Trust?

- Idiots from Hell – Defying Lunatics Among Us

- No More Doubt – Science Confirms the Bible

- Find Peace of Mind or Lose Your Mind

- Fight Back Manual – Last Bet Strategies for Survival of Western Civilization

- Liberals Hijacking America

- Clouds over Beverly Hills

- Several media books (published mostly in Europe)

More information is available @ NeverGiveUpYourDream.US or PierreKandorfer.com

www.ingramcontent.com/pod-product-compliance
Lightning Source LLC
Chambersburg PA
CBHW061815250726
48657CB00001B/443